The St. Nicholas Book

Santa Claus's Rebuke, engraving in *Thomas Nast's Christmas Drawings for the Human Race,* 1890.

The St. Nicholas Book

A CELEBRATION OF CHRISTMAS PAST

Edited by Martin Greif

THE MAIN STREET PRESS · PITTSTOWN, NEW JERSEY

Revised edition 1984

Published by
The Main Street Press, Inc.
William Case House
Pittstown, New Jersey 08867

Distributed in the United States by
Kampmann & Company, Inc.
9 East 40th Street
New York, New York 10016

Published simultaneously in Canada by
Methuen Publications
2330 Midland Avenue
Agincourt, Ontario M1S 1P7

Cover design by Frank Mahood

Printed in the United States of America

Library of Congress Cataloging in Publication Data
Main entry under title:

The St. Nicholas book.

   Summary: A collection of stories, essays, poems, and illustrations from the nineteenth-century juvenile magazine reflecting the Christmas customs of the time.
   1. Christmas—Literary collections. [1. Christmas—Literary collections]
I. Greif, Martin.
PZ5.S17 1985   820'.8'033   84-15460
ISBN 0-915590-51-4 (pbk.)

A Celebration of Christmas Past

"A merry Christmas, uncle! God save you!"
cried a cheerful voice.
"Bah!" said Scrooge, "Humbug!"

A Christmas Carol

Scrooge's "Bah! Humbug!" notwithstanding, most of us share at least one trait in common with Dickens's curmudgeonly antihero. For, like Scrooge before us, we are all—almost to the last of us—haunted by the ghost of Christmas Past. And, as the peal of the yuletide cash register is heard in the land, the ghost of Christmas Past dogs our childhood memories and prods us to a single conclusion: *Christmas is not what it was.* Faced with a battery of plastic Christmas trees, of greasy Santa Clauses with tobacco-stained beards and suits of synthetic polyester and fake white fur, an army of St. Nicks landing by helicopter in the parking lots of suburban shopping centers, of "Silent Night" rocked and rolled so raucously that the very angels hold their ears and laugh or weep, what alternative have we but to reminisce about the joys of Christmas past?

Christmas, we often hear—and *every* generation has heard this lament—is not what it was. There is, of course, demonstrable truth in this judgment. We no longer eat boar's head for Christmas dinner, preferring the blandness (and convenience) of frozen turkey, glutinous and tasteless with packaged stuffing, store-bought mincemeat pie, and canned plum pudding. Nor do we revel before a blazing yule-log (where would we put it?), basking in its warmth and frolicking in the vulgar riot of the season. We accept instead as Christmas cheer the ghostly glare of a flickering television tube, watching with one weary eye the twenty-seventh rerun of the mephitic *Amahl* or a celebrity-laden Christmas-Eve party hosted by Bob Hope, now half again as old as Santa Claus himself. Gathering winter greenery in the final years of the twentieth century means less a journey through the snow-covered woods than a dusty trip to the attic or the closet to retrieve plastic sprigs of mistletoe and artificial sprays of holly, both perfect complements to the three styrofoam Magi plunked like tombstones on the lawn and the rubbery wreath upon the door.

No. Christmas is not what is used to be. But was it ever what we think it was? Hardly.

The ghost of memory plays strange tricks. The belief that Christmas past was somehow glorious—a golden age of simple pleasures and charming innocence—while Christmas present is something considerably less—a moment of leaden commercialism, tarnished and diminished—derives more from a perennial sense of disappointment with what Christmas *is* than from any real recollection of what Christmas *was*. For Christmas almost inevitably disappoints: the day itself is but an anticlimax to weeks of preparation and anticipation. Any climax, of course, would seem pallid after the vast amount of preparation which we devote to the holiday. But even more important to our sense of adult disappointment is the ever-present likelihood of self-delusion. We indulge ourselves in nostalgia, comparing the present day with the Christmases of our childhood, or with the phantoms of what we *think* were our parents' and grandparents' Christmases, finding theirs so terribly rich and our own so terribly wanting. What we recall, in fact, is the intensity of childhood, a day of pleasure, of gifts, of games, of fun—uncomplicated by the need to work, to plan, to save, to cook, to pay the bills. We long for the Christmases of childhood, of sleeping with dancing visions of sugarplums and awakening to dreams fulfilled: where joy exists only in continuous receiving and where one never has to give.

Christmas, then, can no more be what it was when we were children than Santa Claus can retain in middle age the character of life with which childhood has imbued him.

Religious ritual aside, the feast called Christmas, its decorated tree and its orgy of gift-giving, its roast goose or turkey, its greeting cards and its roly-poly Santa, is a relatively recent development, a composite invention of the second quarter of the nineteenth century. Fulfilling the fundamental human desire to cease from work and to rejoice in the dead of winter, just as our pagan ancestors had celebrated the winter solstice long before the birth of Christ, Christmas was slow in developing. And not everyone wanted it, complaining, of course, that even early Christmases were not as holy as they once were—an old complaint. Claiming, and rightly so, that the holiday revels were pagan in origin and that Christmas, consequently, had little to do with Christianity, the Puritans of the English Commonwealth and their brethren in New England banned its celebration. Their experiment in "putting the Christ back in Christmas" was a resounding failure. Eventually, the old paganism—otherwise known as fun and jollity—reestablished itself, stronger than ever. But even by the beginning of the nineteenth century, the iconography of Christmas as we've come to know it was yet nonexistent in England and America. It took the Victorian Age, significantly a period of rampant industrialism, to create that mass nostalgia for "the happy days of yore" so necessary for the communal experience of the modern Christmas.

The institution of Christmas was popularized and sentimentalized by the literary, and not inconsiderably commercial, talents of Charles Dickens, Washington Irving (with an assist from the Reverend Clement Moore) and by the talented pens of Thomas Nast and Sir John Tenniel, and by many other lesser lights. Their ideas and inventions, embellishments and revivals all of customs borrowed from the Celts, the Latins, and the Germans, were disseminated through the stories, poems, and especially the woodcuts of nineteenth-century magazines: *Harper's Weekly, Godey's Lady's Book and Magazine, Frank Leslie's Illustrated Newspaper,* and, for the children, *Harper's Young People, Chatterbox,* and *St. Nicholas.*

Christmas as we've come to know it, then, is a Victorian feast, the all-important Christmas tree itself borrowed from the Germans, popularized by Victoria's consort, the German Prince Albert, and brought to America by Teutonic immigrants. And Santa Claus—his toys and nocturnal visitations across rooftops and down chimneys—was unknown to the English on both shores of the Atlantic before the early nineteenth century. The secularized saint burgeoned suddenly into the childhood hero of Christmas Eve when he and his gift-laden stockings were adopted from German-Americans, completely Americanized (by Moore and Nast), and finally imported back across the sea—to England as Father Christmas, a German immigrant with an American accent, but sufficiently English to be a foreigner in the lands from whence he came.

But the Christmas we have learned to call "an old-fashioned Christmas" is inevitably the creation of one man: Charles Dickens, master storyteller of the Victorian Age. Dickens created a brilliant fantasy of a Christmas that never was, a world of Christmas gaiety and revelry in contradistinction to the cruel realities of his own childhood. And, when his pervasive conviction—*la philosophie de Noël,* one critic has called it—of basic human decency, yuletide festiveness and jollity, and sentimental familial love became world-famous, he exploited it in work after work, in public reading and public lecture, until the day he died. More than mere literary works alone, Dickens created the mythology of Christmas cheer, the never-never-land of Christmas Past that he imagined in order to assuage the actual deprivation of his youth. Beautiful this holiday vision is, charming and delightful, but no more "real" than last year's Christmas cards or this year's minuscule dividends in the Christmas Club account.

A century after Dickens's first work appeared, Irving Berlin, an unlikely successor, dreamed of a white Christmas "just like the ones [he] used to know," and millions and millions of sentimental people, preconditioned by Dickens, bought records, spreading holiday cheer and lucre, and participating in the economy of the burgeoning Christmas industry. Dickensian Christmases are, of course, invariably white, Christmas-card white, Currier & Ives white. Soft the snow, tender its fall, perfect for the likes of Frosty the Snowman and even Rudolf with his nose so red. Waves of nostalgia wash over us, snowflakes clouding our vision and our reason. Imagining Christmas revels before a roaring fire, we ignore the realities of Christmas past, of a Dickensian yule untouched by the purveyors of seasonal kitsch. "*Sunday, Christmas Day 1870,*" a country parson notes in his diary, a *real* diary, of a *real* Christmas:

Sunday, Christmas Day 1870. As I lay awake praying in the early morning I thought I heard a sound of distant bells. It was an intense frost. I sat down in my bath upon a sheet of thick ice which broke in the middle into large pieces while sharp points and jagged edges stuck all round the sides of the tub like *chevaux de frise,* not particularly comforting to the naked thighs and loins, for the keen ice cut like broken glass. The ice water stung and scorched like fire. I had to collect the floating pieces of ice and pile them on a chair before I could use the sponge and then I had to thaw the sponge in my hands for it was a mass of ice.

This is Christmas, an old-fashioned Christmas, if you will—but not the stuff that popular tunes or the cloying verse on Christmas cards are made of. The scene, however, is refreshing, the icy water of the holiday bath, the numbed skin and chilled bones of the shivering parson suggesting immediately why the nostalgic vision of Christmas past accentuates its quintessential *warmth.* We recollect imagined warmth to relieve the chilblains of growing up, of realizing with reconciled disappointment, a pervasive disappointment, that Christmas is for children.

And yet, disappointment or no, there is consolation in knowing that *every* generation has felt the same way. Each age has complained that Christmas is not what it was. As Parson Kilvert was shuddering in his bath in the winter of 1870, an anonymous poet was penning his grown-up lament and calling it "The Cynic's Carol":

> Tradition calls for snow—no snow today;
> Only the old abuses in the old, old way:
> Mendicants cry, Give! and debtors, Wait! and credit, Pay!
>   Because it's Christmas!
>
> Some one brings tokening plush and celluloid,
> Of use or beauty, sentiment or soul, devoid,
> With fond but fatuous hope I shall be overjoyed,
>   Because it's Christmas!
>
> A dame whose whim is to propitiate,
> Sends me a china rooster filled with chocolate
> Nougat, or some confection I abominate,
>   Because it's Christmas!

Or, as Ogden Nash put it three-quarters of a century later: "Roses are things which Christmas is not a bed of them. . . ." The story is drearily familiar: disappointment in growing up, and yearning for the uncomplicated pleasures of childhood when everything was wonderful—except to the parents and grandparents, who knew otherwise.

Enough. As you leaf through the pages of this book, you can indulge yourselves in a nostalgic return to a Victorian Christmas, when everything about the yuletide was pure and wholesome and beautiful—or so it seemed. The old lithographs, the poems, the passages of prose allow us to relive the transport of a dream, to reexperience a perfect Christmas, unblemished by the realities of adult cares. But as we allow outselves to be wafted back to a world of Dickensian innocence, we must not betray what even children know: that we must awaken from all dreams. Christmas, perfect *this* year, will be somehow different *next* year. The young readers of *St. Nicholas* magazine knew this full well in the winter of 1889, when Julie M. Lippmann warned about the coming of "A New-Fashioned Christmas," when a "modern" Santa Claus, dressed in the latest fashionable vogue— and sporting spats, a monocle, and a cane—would travel by elevated railway and send his gifts by express:

> I ran to him and begged him, between
>   my sobs and tears,
> To leave us blessed Christmas, just as in
>   former years.
> To change no little custom; to take no
>   part away;
> To leave us dear old-fashioned, beloved
>   Christmas Day.

Almost a century ago, Miss Lippmann, begging Santa to leave things as they were, awakened triumphant from her dream, finding Christmas just as she had remembered it. As Santa lands his helicopter again this year amidst the traffic in the supermarket parking lot, will we awaken from ours?

Merry Christmas

M for the   Music, merry and clear;
E for the   Eve, the crown of the year;
R for the   Romping of bright girls and boys;
R for the   Reindeer that bring them the toys;
Y for the   Yule-log softly aglow.

C for the   Cold of the sky and the snow;
H for the   Hearth where they hang up the hose;
R for the   Reel which the old folk propose;
I for the   Icicles seen through the pane;
S for the   Sleigh-bells, with tinkling refrain;
T for the   Tree with gifts all a-bloom;
M for the   Mistletoe hung in the room;
A for the   Anthems we all love to hear;
S for   ST. Nicholas—joy of the year!

St. Nicholas (January, 1897)

German Christmas postcard, c. 1900.

What Does Johnny Want?

DEAR SANTA CLAUS:

I don't want a thing that girls would like;
I don't want a velocipede, but a bike;
I don't want a gun that will not shoot;
I don't want an engine that won't toot;
I don't want mittens for the snow;
I don't want a horse-car that won't go;
I don't want anything to wear;
I don't want an apple or a pear;
I don't want anything made of tin;
I don't want a top that will not spin;
I don't want any book I can't use;
I don't want a best pair of shoes;
I don't want a ship that won't sail;
I don't want a goody-goody tale;
I don't want a game that I can't play;
I don't want a donkey that won't bray;
I don't want a small fish pond like Fred's;
I don't want one of those baby sleds;
I don't want paints that are no good;
I don't want building-blocks of wood;
I don't want *you* to think I am queer;
Nor I don't want you to think I don't want anything this year.

    Yours truly,
    JOHNNY.

P.S.—I was just about not to say,
I don't want you to forget me Christmas Day.

Montrose J. Moses
St. Nicholas (December, 1899)

Christmas Post, engraving by Thomas Nast in
Harper's Weekly, January 4, 1879.

The Story of the Holly Sprig

"I'd be the shiniest green,"
  Wished once a sprig of holly,
"That e'er a Yule was seen,
  And deck some banquet jolly!"

"I'd be the cheeriest red,"
  Wished once the holly-berry,
"That e'er at board rich spread
  Helped make the feasters merry!"

In a little market stall
  At Yule the sprig lay waiting,
For fine folk one and all
  Passed by that open grating.

The Eve of Christmas Day
  It had been passed by many,
When one turned not away
  And bought it for a penny.

Hers was a home of care
  Which not a wreath made jolly;
The only Christmas there
  Was that sweet sprig of holly.

"Oh, this is better far
  Than banquet!" thought the berry;
The leaves glowed like a star
  And made that cottage merry!

Arthur Upson
St. Nicholas (December, 1907)

The Holly Cart, lithograph by E. Duncan after a painting by George C. Leighton, 1856.

Santa Claus's Correspondents

Eighteen letters for Santa Claus were received at the New York post-office one morning. No two were directed exactly alike. The first was the most direct, and was the only one in which a definite address was given. Here it is:

> MR. SANTA CLAUS
> 444 Cherry Street,
> New York

This was written in a scrawling hand, but the number was quite plain. It was probably the only one of the lot that did not go directly to the dead-letter office. There was the name, a definite number on a definite street in a definite city, and in the lower left-hand corner was the regular United States two-cent postage-stamp. So the letter was given to the proper carrier, who took it to the Cherry Street address. When it came back, this legend was stamped in red ink across the face:

> REMOVED: PRESENT ADDRESS UNKNOWN.

There is something realistic in the word "removed." It shows at least that the post-office folks are not skeptical in the belief that Santa Claus *had* his home at 444 Cherry Street. If this be true, some young persons will think it was very careless of the old gentleman not to leave his new address. But he is so busy at this time of the year that he may have forgotten it.

One letter came folded and turned down at one corner, and the stamp was placed so as to hold the folded corner down. It read as follows:

> DEAR MR. SANTA CLAUS: I only want a pare of skates for Christmas
> and if it aint cold a sled will do. My old ones bust. If they aint
> no snow I would like anything you think of. My mamma says you are
> poor this year.
> Yours truly. . . .

The New York Exchange (December, 1893)

Santa Claus's Mail, engraving in *Thomas Nast's Christmas Drawings for the Human Race,* 1890.

About Santa Claus

Santa Claus lives somewhere near the North Pole, so he can't be interfered with. It is the only place where he can be sure of not being overrun with callers, who would take up all his time, and prevent him from getting his Christmas budget ready—by no means a light piece of work. As to how he makes up his load of toys, it is certainly curious; but it is his business not ours. He uses reindeer to draw his sleigh because no other animals can endure the climate in which their master must live. Just what the Saint looks like is not altogether certain, but there is a belief among the children who have sat up to receive his visits that he is not so big but that he can get through an ordinary chimney; that he is compelled to dress in furs because of the cold ride through the long winter night; that he looks good-natured because no one that loves young folk can help looking so; and that his beard and his hair are white because he is older by some years than he was in his younger days. He must be a jolly and kindly old gentleman, for otherwise he wouldn't be giving out his toys in that sly, queer way of his—after the little ones are fast asleep and snug in their beds. Oh, we can tell quite a number of things about his tricks and his manners! But don't sit up for him; he doesn't like it. He loses valuable time when he is compelled to dodge the prying eyes of little Susan Sly and Master Paul Pry, and so kindly an old fellow should not be bothered. Just go to bed, close your eyes up good and tight, and—see what you will find in the morning!

St. Nicholas (December, 1899)

A Merry Christmas and Happy New Year, unsigned lithograph in
Harper's Weekly, January 2, 1869

Returning Home with the Spoils

Oh! we've all been shopping, shop, shop, shopping,
 We've bought our Christmas gifts, and had a tiresome promenade;
And we're all of us a-dropping, drop, drop, dropping
 Fast asleep, except papa, that idle man, who only paid.

When we were busy choosing, choose, choose, choosing,
 He merely yawned at intervals behind his *porte-monnaie;*
So now while we are losing, lose, lose, losing
 Ourselves in dreams, he's wide awake—he only had to pay.

Anonymous poem in *Harper's Bazaar*
(January 6, 1877)

Returning Home with the Spoils, engraving by H. Harral
in *Harper's Bazaar,* January 6, 1877.

A Christmas Family-Party

Who can be insensible to the outpourings of good feeling, and the honest interchange of affectionate attachment, which abound at this season of the year? A Christmas family-party! We know nothing in nature more delightful! There seems a magic in the very name of Christmas. Petty jealousies and discords are forgotten; social feelings are awakened, in bosoms to which they have long been strangers; father and son, or brother and sister, who have met and passed with averted gaze, or a look of cold recognition, for months before, proffer and return the cordial embrace, and bury their past animosities in their present happiness. Kindly hearts that have yearned towards each other but have been withheld by false notions of pride and self-dignity, are again reunited, and all is kindness and benevolence! Would that Christmas lasted the whole year through (as it ought), and that the prejudices and passions which deform our better nature, were never called into action among those to whom they should ever be strangers!

from *Sketches by Boz* (1836) by Charles Dickens

Visit to the Old Folks on Christmas Eve,
hand-colored lithograph for American export by
B. Dondorf, Berlin, c. 1875.

Bringing Christmas Home

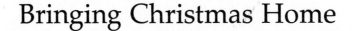

Life still hath one romance that naught can bury—
Not Time himself, who coffins Life's romances—
For still will Christmas gild the year's mischances,
If Childhood comes, as here, to make him merry.

From *The Christmas Tree* by Thomas
Watts-Dunton (c.1900)

The Christmas Tree, lithograph after a painting by E. Osborn, 1864.

A Letter To Santa Claus

I've written a letter to Santa Claus;
  Would you like to know the reason?
'Tis very plain and just because
  We've moved this present season.
I'm always called a happy child,
  Yet for weeks I've had this worry—
Will Santa Claus know that we're here,
  Or pass us in his hurry?

I told him not to pass us by,
  And gave our street and number—
He cannot tell by faces; why?
  He comes while we all slumber;
Besides, I've had some other fears—
  Our chimney is so narrow
It will not hold old Santa's wares,
  It scarce would hold a barrow.

I've given him quite a list of things;
  Of dolls and little dishes,
Of skates and sleds, and kites and strings,
  And many other wishes;
I said, "Dear Santa, please do come,
  Nor mind the narrow passage,
For every child within the home
  Has sent to you this message."

Anna D. Walker (c. 1890)

Game of the Visit of Santa Claus, produced by
McLaughlin Bros., New York, 1897.

A December Ditty

The Holly, oh, the Holly!
  Green leaf, and berry red,
Is the plant that thrives in winter
  When all the rest are fled.
When snows are on the ground,
  And the skies are gray and drear
The Holly comes at Christmas-tide
  And brings the Christmas cheer.
Sing the Mistletoe, the Ivy,
  And the Holly-bush so gay,
That comes to us in winter—
  No summer friends are they.

Give me the sturdy friendship
  That will ever loyal hold,
And give me the hardy Holly
  That dares the winter's cold;
Oh, the roses bloom in June,
  When the skies are bright and clear,
But the Holly comes at Christmas-tide
  The best time o' the year.
Sing the Holly, and the Ivy,
  And the merry Mistletoe,
That come to us in winter
  When the fields are white with snow!

Alice Williams Brotherton
St. Nicholas (January, 1891)

Making Christmas Garlands, engraving by C.D. Weldon
in *Harper's Young People,* December 15, 1885.

A Visit from St. Nicholas

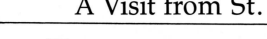

'Twas the night before Christmas, when all through the house
Not a creature was stirring, not even a mouse;
The stockings were hung by the chimney with care;
In hopes that St. Nicholas soon would be there;
The children were nestled all snug in their beds,
While visions of sugarplums danced in their heads;
And mamma in her kerchief and I in my cap
Had just settled our brains for a long winter's nap
When out on the lawn there arose such a clatter,
I sprang from my bed to see what was the matter.
Away to the window I flew like a flash,
Tore open the shutters, and threw up the sash;
The moon, on the breast of the new-fallen snow,
Gave a luster of midday to objects below;
When what to my wondering eyes should appear
But a miniature sleigh and eight tiny reindeer,
With a little old driver, so lively and quick,
I knew in a moment, it must be St. Nick.
More rapid than eagles his coursers they came,
And he whistled and shouted and called them by name:
"Now Dasher! now Dancer! now Prancer! now Vixen!
On, Comet! on, Cupid! on, Donner and Blitzen!
To the top of the porch! To the top of the wall!
Now, dash away, dash away, dash away, all!"
As dry leaves that before the wild hurricane fly,
When they meet with an obstacle, mount to the sky,
So up to the housetop the coursers they flew,
With the sleigh full of toys and St. Nicholas too.
And then, in a twinkling, I heard on the roof
The prancing and pawing of each little hoof.
As I drew in my head and was turning around,
Down the chimney St. Nicholas came with a bound.
He was dressed all in fur from his head to his foot,
And his clothes were all tarnished with ashes and soot;
A bundle of toys he had flung on his back,
And he looked like a peddler just opening his pack.
His eyes: how they twinkled! his dimples: how merry!

His cheeks were like roses, his nose like a cherry;
His droll little mouth was drawn up like a bow,
And the beard on his chin was as white as the snow.
The stump of a pipe he held tight in his teeth,
And the smoke, it encircled his head like a wreath:
He had a broad face, and a little round belly,
That shook, when he laughed, like a bowl full of jelly;
He was chubby and plump, a right jolly old elf;
And I laughed when I saw him, in spite of myself;
A wink of his eye and a twist of his head
Soon gave me to know I had nothing to dread.
He spoke not a word, but went straight to his work
And filled all the stockings; then turned with a jerk,
And laying his finger aside of his nose,
And giving a nod, up the chimney he rose.
He sprang to his sleigh, to his team gave a whistle,
And away they all flew like the down of a thistle;
But I heard him exclaim, ere he drove out of sight,
"Happy Christmas to all, and to all a good night!"

Clement Clarke Moore
(December, 1823)

Christmas postcard, c. 1900.

Christmas in the Heart

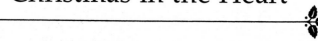

It is Christmas in the mansion,
  Yule-log fires and silken frocks:
It is Christmas in the cottage,
  Mother's filling little socks.

It is Christmas on the highway,
  In the thronging, busy mart;
But the dearest, truest Christmas
  Is the Christmas in the heart.

Anonymous

A Chance to Test Santa Claus's Generosity, engraving in
Thomas Nast's Christmas Drawings for the Human Race, 1890.

The Angel's Story

Through the blue and frosty heavens
  Christmas stars were shining bright;
Glistening lamps throughout the city
  Almost matched their gleaming light;
While the winter snow was lying,
And the winter winds were sighing,
  Long ago, one Christmas night.

While from every tower and steeple
  Pealing bells were sounding clear,
(Never were such tones of gladness
  Save when Christmas time is near),
Many a one that night was merry
  Who had toiled through all the year.

That night saw old wrongs forgiven,
  Friends, long parted, reconciled;
Voices all unused to laughter,
  Mournful eyes that rarely smiled,
Trembling hearts that feared the morrow,
  From their anxious thoughts beguiled.

Rich and poor felt love and blessing
  From the gracious season fall;
Joy and plenty in the cottage,
  Peace and feasting in the hall;
And the voices of the children
  Ringing clear above it all!

Adelaide Anne Procter (c.1858)

German Christmas postcard, c. 1900.

If You're Good

Santa Claus'll come to-night,
  If you're *good*,
And do what you know is right,
  As you should;
Down the chimney he will creep,
Bringing you a wooly sheep,
And a doll that goes to sleep;—
  If you're *good*.

Santa Claus will drive his sleigh
  Thro' the wood,
But he'll come around this way
  If you're *good*,
With a wind-up bird that sings,
And a puzzle made of rings—
Jumping-jacks and funny things—
  If you're *good*.

Santa grieves when you are bad,
  As he should;
But it makes him very glad
  When you're *good*.
He is wise, and he's a dear;
Just do right and never fear;
He'll remember you each year,
  If you're *good*.

James Courtney Challiss
St. Nicholas (December, 1896)

The Same Old Christmas Story Over Again,
engraving in *Thomas Nast's Christmas Drawings
for the Human Race,* 1890.

Early Christmas Morning

Four little feet pattering on the floor,
Two tangled curly heads peeping at the door,
Hear the merry laughter, happy childish roar,
     Early Christmas morning.

Two little stockings full of sweets and toys,
Everything charming for little girls and boys.
How could they help, then, making such a noise?
     Early Christmas morning.

Down beside the stockings many gifts were spread,
Dollies, drums, a cradle and a brand new sled.
"Haven't we too many?" little Nellie said,
     Early Christmas morning.

Four little bare feet on the sidewalk cold,
Two little faces with want and hunger old
Peeping through the window where those gifts unrolled,
     Early Christmas morning.

"Yes," says John to Nellie, as he spied the two,
"We've so many presents, tell you what we'll do.
I'll give half of mine away. Now, dear Nell, will you?"
     Early Christmas morning.

Two little famished ones in the house were called,
Favors heaped upon them till they stood enthralled.
Was not this the angel's song, "Peace, good-will to all?"
     Early Christmas morning.

Mary B. Peck

St. Nicholas, hand-colored lithograph for
American export by B. Dondorf, Berlin, c. 1875.

Welcome to Christmas

He comes—the brave old Christmas!
  His sturdy steps I hear;
We will give him a hearty welcome,
  For he comes but once a year!

And of all our old acquaintance
  'Tis he we like the best;
There's a jolly old way about him—
  There's a warm heart in his breast.

He is not too proud to enter
  Your house though it be mean;
Yet is company fit for a courtier,
  And is welcomed by the Queen!

He can tell you a hundred stories
  Of the Old World's whims and ways,
And how they merrily wish'd him joy
  In our fathers' courting days.

He laughs with the heartiest laughter
  That does one good to hear;
'Tis a pity so brave an old fellow
  Should come but once a year!

But once, then, let us be ready,
  With all that he can desire—
With plenty of holly and ivy,
  And a huge log for the fire;

With plenty of noble actions,
  And plenty of warm good-will;
With our hearts as full of kindness
  As the board we mean to fill.

With plenty of store in the larder,
  And plenty of wine in the bin;
And plenty of mirth for the kitchen;
  Then open and let him in!

Oh, he is a fine old fellow—
  His heart's in the truest place;
You may know that at once by the
    children,
  Who glory to see his face.

from *Welcome to Christmas*
by Mary Howitt (c. 1870)

Christmas Station, engraved in *Thomas Nast's Christmas Drawings for the Human Race*, 1890.

Sing We All Merrily

Sing we all merrily
   Christmas is here,
The day that we love best
   Of days in the year.

Bring forth the holly,
   The box, and the bay,
Deck out our cottage
   For glad Christmas Day.

Sing we all merrily,
   Draw around the fire,
Sister and brother,
   Grandsire, and sire.

Anonymous

German Christmas postcard, c. 1910.

A Christmas Eve Thought

If Santa Claus should stumble,
  As he climbs the chimney tall
With all this ice upon it,
  I'm afraid he'd get a fall
And smash himself to pieces—
  To say nothing of the toys!
Dear me, what sorrow that would bring
  To all the girls and boys!
So I am going to write a note
  And pin it to the gate,—
I'll write it large, so he can see,
  No matter if it's late,—
And say, "Dear Santa Claus, don't try
  To climb the roof to-night,
But walk right in, the door's unlocked,
  The nursery's on the right!"

Harriot Brewer Sterling
St. Nicholas (December, 1895)

St. Claus, lithograph by S. Merinsky, New York, 1872.

Is There a Santa Claus?

. . . Yes, Virginia, there *is* a Santa Claus. He exists as certainly as love and generosity and devotion exist, and you know that they abound and give to your life its highest beauty and joy. Alas! how dreary would be the world if there were no Santa Claus! It would be as dreary as if there were no Virginias. There would be no childlike faith then, no poetry, no romance to make tolerable this existence. We should have no enjoyment, except in sense and sight. The eternal light with which childhood fills the world would be extinguished.

Not believe in Santa Claus! You might as well not believe in fairies! You might get your papa to hire men to watch in all the chimneys on Christmas Eve to catch Santa Claus, but even if they did not see Santa Claus coming down, what would that prove? Nobody sees Santa Claus, but that is no sign that there is no Santa Claus. The most real things in the world are those that no children or men can see. Did you ever see fairies dancing on the lawn? Of course not, but that's no proof that they are not there. Nobody can conceive or imagine all the wonders there are unseen or unseeable in the world . . . .

No Santa Claus! Thank God he lives, and he lives forever. A thousand years from now, Virginia, nay, ten times ten thousand years from now, he will continue to make glad the heart of childhood.

Francis P. Church's editorial in *The New York Sun*
(September 21, 1897) in response to a letter
from eight-year-old Virginia O'Hanlon

Christmas postcard, c. 1905.

Santa's Toys

Santa Claus was driving his reindeer, his teeming sleigh filled with wonders from every region: dolls that walked and talked and sang, fit for princesses; sleds fine enough for princes; drums and trumpets and swords for young heroes; horses that looked as though they were alive and would spring next moment from their rockers; bats and balls that almost started of themselves from their places; little uniforms, and frocks; skates; tennis-racquets; baby caps and rattles; tiny engines and coaches; railway trains; animals that ran about; steamships; books; pictures—everything to delight the soul of childhood and gratify the affection of age. . . .

from *Santa Claus's Partner* (1899)
by Thomas Nelson Page

Merry Old Santa Claus, engraving by Thomas Nast
in *Harper's Weekly,* January 1, 1881.

A Christmas Alphabet

A is for Animals who shared the stable.
B is for the Babe with their manger for cradle.
C is for the Carols so blithe and so gay.
D for December, the twenty-fifth day.
E for the Eve when we're all so excited.
F for the Fun when the tree's at last lighted.
G is the Goose which you all know is fat.
H for the Holly you stick in your hat.
I for the Ivy that clings to the wall.
J is for Jesus, the cause of it all.
K for the Kindness begot by this feast.
L is the Light shining way in the east.
M for the Mistletoe, all green and white.
N for the Nowells we sing Christmas night.
O for the Oxen, the first to adore Him.
P for the Presents Wise Men laid before Him.
Q for the Queerness that this should have been
　　Near two thousand years before you were seen.
R for the Reindeer leaping the roofs.
S for the Stockings that Santa Claus stuffs.
T for the Toys, the Tinsel, the Tree.
U is for Us—the whole family.
V is for Visitors bringing us cheer.
W is Welcome to the happy New Year.
X **Y Z** bother me! All I can say,
　　Is this is the end of my Christmas lay.
　　So now to you all, wherever you be,
　　A merry, merry Christmas, and many may you see!

Anonymous (c. 1890)

English Christmas postcard, c. 1910.

Santa Claus

He comes in the night! He comes in the night!
  He softly, silently comes,
While the little brown heads on the pillows so white
  Are dreaming of bugles and drums.
He cuts thro' the snow like a ship thro' the foam,'
  While the white flakes 'round him whirl.
Who tells him I know not, but he findeth the home
  Of each good little boy and girl.

His sleigh it is long, and deep, and wide;
  It will carry a host of things,
While dozens of drums hang over the side,
  With the sticks sticking under the strings.
And yet not the sound of a drum is heard,
  Not a bugle blast is blown,
As he mounts to the chimney-top like a bird,
  And drops to the hearth like a stone.

The little red stockings he silently fills,
  Till the stockings will hold no more;
The bright little sleds for the great snow hills
  Are quickly set down on the floor.
Then Santa Claus mounts to the roof like a bird,
  And glides to his seat in the sleigh;
Not the sound of a bugle or drum is heard
  As he noiselessly gallops away.

Anonymous (c. 1880)

The Coming of Santa Claus, engraving in *Thomas Nast's Christmas Drawings for the Human Race*, 1890.

Christmas

They put me in the great spare bed, and there they bade me sleep:
I must not stir; I must not wake; I must not even peep!
Right opposite that lonely bed, my Christmas stocking hung;
While near it, waiting for the morn, my Sunday clothes were flung.

I counted softly, to myself, to ten, and ten times ten,
And went through all the alphabet, and then began again;
I repeated that Fifth Reader piece—a poem called "Repose,"
And tried a dozen other ways to fall into a doze—
When suddenly the room grew light. I heard a soft, strong bound—
'Twas Santa Claus, I felt quite sure, but dared not look around,
'Twas nice to know that he was there, and things were going rightly,
And so I took a little nap, and tried to smile politely.

"Ho! Merry Christmas!" cried a voice; I felt the bed a-rocking;
'Twas daylight—Brother Bob was up! and oh, that splendid stocking!

Bessie Hill
St. Nicholas (December, 1889)

Christmas Morning: Before Daylight, lithograph
by the Kellogg and Bulkley Co., Hartford, c. 1870

A Dear Little Schemer

There was a little daughter once, whose feet were—oh, so small!
That when the Christmas Eve came 'round, they wouldn't do at all.
At least she said they wouldn't do, and so she tried another's,
And folding her wee stocking up, she slyly took her mother's.

"I'll pin this big one here," she said,—then sat before the fire,
Watching the supple, dancing flames, and shadows darting by her,
Till silently she drifted of to that queer land, you know,
Of "Nowhere in particular," where sleepy children go.

She never knew the tumult rare that came upon the roof!
She never heard the patter of a single reindeer hoof;
She never knew how Some One came and looked his shrewd surprise
At the wee foot and the stocking—so different in size!

She only knew, when morning dawned, that she was safe in bed.
"It's Christmas! Ho"—and merrily she raised her pretty head;
Then, wild with glee, she saw what "dear Old Santa Claus" had done,
And ran to tell the joyful news to each and every one!

"Mama! Papa! Please come and look! a lovely doll, and all!"
And "See how full the stocking is! Mine *would* have been too small.
I borrowed this for Santa Claus. It isn't fair, you know,
To make him wait forever for a little girl to grow."

Mary Mapes Dodge
St. Nicholas (December, 1887)

The Dream Realized, engraving by W. Thomas in
The Graphic, December 25, 1869.

Christmas Morning

On Christmas Day, when fires were lit,
  And all our breakfasts done,
We spread our toys out on the floor
  And played there in the sun.

The nursery smelled of Christmas tree,
  And under where it stood
The shepherds watched their flocks of sheep,
  —All made of painted wood.

Outside the house the air was cold
  And quiet all about,
Till far across the snowy roofs
  The Christmas bells rang out.

But soon the sleigh-bells jingled by
  Upon the street below,
And people on the way to church,
  Went crunching through the snow.

We did not quarrel once all day;
  Mama and Grandma said
They liked to be in where we were,
  So pleasantly we played.

I do not see how any child
  Is cross on Christmas day,
When all the lovely toys are new,
  And everyone can play.

Katharine Pyle
St. Nicholas (December, 1890)

Christmas Morning, lithograph signed J. F., New York, c. 1890.

Holiday Presents

She had a splendid Christmas. She went to bed early, so as to let Santa Claus have a chance at the stockings, and in the morning she was up the first of anybody and went and felt them, and found hers all lumpy with packages of candy, and oranges and grapes, and pocket-books and rubber balls and all kinds of small presents, and her big brother's with nothing but the tongs in them, and her young lady sister's with a new silk umbrella, and her papa's and mama's with potatoes and pieces of coal wrapped up in tissue paper, just as they always had every Christmas. Then she waited around till the rest of the family were up, and she was the first to burst into the library, when the doors were opened, and look at the large presents laid out on the library-table—books, and portfolios, and boxes of stationery, and breast-pins, and dolls, and little stoves, and dozens of handkerchiefs, and ink-stands, and skates, and snow-shovels, and photograph-frames, and little easels, and boxes of water-colors, and Turkish paste, and nougat, and candied cherries, and dolls' houses, and waterproofs,—and the big Christmas-tree lighted and standing in a waste-basket in the middle.

She had a splendid Christmas all day. She ate so much candy that she did not want any breakfast; and the whole forenoon the presents kept pouring in that the expressman had not had time to deliver the night before; and she went 'round giving the presents she had got for other people, and came home and ate turkey and cranberry for dinner, and plum-pudding and nuts and raisins and oranges and more candy, and then went out and coasted and came in with a stomach-ache, crying . . .

from "Christmas Every Day" by William Dean Howells,
St. Nicholas (January, 1886)

Holiday Presents, lithograph by Kimmel & Voigt, 1871.

Christmas Thoughts

Of all the old festivals, that of Christmas awakens the strongest and most heart-felt associations. There is a tone of solemn and sacred feeling that blends with our conviviality and lifts the spirit to a state of hallowed and elevated enjoyment.

It is a beautiful arrangement, derived from days of yore, that this festival, which commemorates the announcement of the religion of peace and love, has been made the season for gathering together of family connections, and drawing closer again those bands of kindred hearts which the cares, and pleasures, and sorrows of the world are continually operating to cast loose; of calling back the children of a family, who have launched forth in life, once more to assemble about the paternal hearth, there to grow young and loving again among the endearing mementos of childhood.

There is something in the very season of the year that gives a charm to the festivity of Christmas. In the depth of winter, when Nature lies despoiled of her charms, wrapt in her shroud of sheeted snow, we turn for our gratifications to moral sources. Heart calleth unto heart, and we draw our pleasures from the deep wells of living kindness which lie in the quiet recesses of our bosoms.

Amidst the general call to happiness, the bustle of the spirits and stir of the affections, which prevail at this period, what bosom can remain insensible? It is indeed the season of regenerated feeling—the season for kindling not merely the fire of hospitality in the hall, but the genial flame of charity in the heart. He who can turn churlishly away from contemplating the felicity of his fellow-beings and can sit down repining in loneliness, when all around is joyful, wants the genial and social sympathies which constitute the charm of a merry Christmas.

from *The Sketch-Book*.
by Washington Irving (1819-20)

Christmas postcard, c. 1900.

Merry Christmas, Every One!

In the rush of the merry morning,
    When the red burns through the gray,
And the wintry world lies waiting
    For the glory of the day,
Then we hear a fitful rushing
    Just without, upon the stair,
See two white phantoms coming,
    Catch the gleam of sunny hair.

Rosy feet upon the threshold,
    Eager faces peeping through,
With the first red ray of sunshine
    Chanting cherubs come in view;
Mistletoe and gleaming holly,
    Symbols of a blessed day,
In their chubby hands they carry,
    Streaming all along the way.

Well we know them, never weary
    Of their innocent surprise;
Waiting, watching, listening always
    With full hearts and tender eyes,
While our little household angels,
    White and golden in the sun.
Greet us with the sweet old welcome—
    "Merry Christmas, every one!"

Anonymous (c. 1868)

Christmas Morning, unsigned engraving in
Harper's Weekly, December, 1864.

Christmas Gifts

Ten Christmas presents standing in a line;
Robert took the bicycle, then there were nine.
Nine Christmas presents ranged in order straight;
Bob took the steam-engine, then there were eight.
Eight Christmas presents—and one came from Devon;
Robbie took the jack-knife, then there were seven.
Seven Christmas presents direct from St. Nick's;
Bobby took the candy-box, then there were six.
Six Christmas presents, one of them alive;
Rob took the puppy-dog, then there were five.
Five Christmas presents yet on the floor;
Bobbin took the soldier-cap, then there were four.
Four Christmas presents underneath the tree;
Bobbet took the writing-desk, then there were three.
Three Christmas presents still in full view;
Robin took the checker-board, then there were two.
Two Christmas presents, promising fun,
Bobbles took the picture-book, and there was one.
One Christmas present—and now the list is done;
Bobbinet took the sled, and then there were none.
And the same happy child received every toy,
So many nicknames had one little boy.

Carolyn Wells
St. Nicholas (January, 1899)

Merry Christmas, lithograph by Thomas Nast
in *Harper's Weekly,* January 4, 1879.

The Christmas Spirit

What is the Christmas spirit?

It is the spirit which brings a smile to the lips and tenderness to the heart; it is the spirit which warms one into friendship with all the world, which impels one to hold out the hand of fellowship to every man and woman.

For the Christmas motto is "Peace on earth, good-will to men," and the spirit of Christmas demands that it ring in our hearts and find expression in kindly acts and loving words.

What a joyful thing for the world it would be if the Christmas spirit could do this, not only on that holiday, but on every day of the year. What a beautiful place the world would be to live in! Peace and good-will everywhere and always! Let each one of us resolve that, so far as we are concerned, peace and good-will shall be our motto every day, and that we will do our best to make the Christmas spirit last all the year round.

Anonymous

A New Suit for Christmas, engraving after a painting by H. Werner
in *Harper's Bazaar*, January 11, 1879.

A Christmas Carol

The old north breeze through the skeleton trees
 Is chanting the year out drearily;
But loud let it blow, for at home we know
 That the dry logs crackle cheerily;
And the frozen ground is in fetters bound;
 But pile up the wood, we can burn it;
For Christmas is come, and in every home
 To summer our hearts can turn it.
   Wassail! wassail!
 Here's happiness to all, for Christmas is come.

Let us drink to those eyes we most dearly prize,
 We can show how we love them after;
The fire blaze cleaves to the bright holly leaves,
 And the mistletoe hangs from the rafter.
We care not for fruit, whilst we here can see
 Their scarlet and pearly berries;
For the girls' soft cheeks shall our peaches be,
 And their pouting lips our cherries.
   Wassail! wassail!
 Here's happiness to all, abroad and at home,
   Wassail! wassail!
 Here's happiness to all, for Christmas is come.

Albert Smith (c. 1850)

Caroling at Christmastide, hand-colored lithograph for
American export by B. Dondorf, Berlin, c. 1875.

A Christmas Tree

I have been looking at a merry company of children assembled round that pretty German toy, a Christmas Tree. The tree was planted in the middle of a great round table, and towered high above their heads. It was brilliantly lighted by a multitude of little tapers; and everywhere sparkled and glittered with bright objects. There were rosy-cheeked dolls, hiding behind the green leaves; and there were real watches (with movable hands, at least, and an endless capacity of being wound up) dangling from innumerable twigs; there were French-polished tables, chairs, bedsteads, wardrobes, eight-day clocks, and various other articles of domestic furniture (wonderfully made in tin), perched among the boughs, as if in preparation for some fairy housekeeping; there were jolly, broad-faced little men, much more agreeable in appearance than many real men—and no wonder, for their heads took off, and showed them to be full of sugar-plums; there were trinkets for the elder girls, far brighter than any grown-up gold and jewels; there were baskets and pincushions in all devices; there were guns, swords, and banners; there were witches standing in enchanted rings of pasteboard, to tell fortunes; there were teetotums, humming-tops, needle-cases, pen-wipers, smelling-bottles, conversation-cards, bouquet-holders; real fruit, made artificially dazzling with gold leaf; imitation apples, pears, and walnuts, crammed with surprises; in short, as a pretty child, before me, delightedly whispered to another pretty child, her bosom friend, "There was everything, and more."

"A Christmas Tree" by Charles Dickens
Household Words (December 21, 1850)

The Christmas Tree, unsigned engraving in *Godey's Lady's Book,* December, 1861.

The Christmas Pudding

In a household where there are five or six children, the eldest not above ten or eleven, the making of the pudding is indeed an event. It is thought of days, if not weeks, before. To be allowed to share in the noble work, is a prize for young ambition. . . . Lo! the lid is raised, curiosity stands on tip-toe, eyes sparkle with anticipation, little hands are clapped in ecstasy, almost too great to find expression in words. "The hour arrives—the moment wished and feared;"—wished, oh! how intensely; feared, not in the event, but lest envious fate should not allow it to be an event, and mar the glorious concoction in its very birth.

And then when it is dished, when all fears of this kind are over, when the roast beef has been removed, when the pudding, in all the glory of its own splendour, shines upon the table, how eager is the anticipation of the near delight! How beautifully it steams! How delicious it smells! How round it is! A kiss is round, the horizon is round, the earth is round, the moon is round, the sun and stars, and all the host of heaven are round. So is plum pudding.

Illustrated London News (December, 1848)

The Christmas Pudding, unsigned engraving in
The Workman, January, 1875.

The Mistletoe

It was after the maze and mirth of the dance,
  Where a spray of green mistletoe swayed,
That I met—and I vow that the meeting was chance!—
  With a very adorable maid.

I stood for a moment in tremor of doubt,
  Then kissed her, half looking for war:
But—"Why did you wait, Sir!" she said, with a pout,
  "Pray, what is the mistletoe for?"

Clinton Scollard (c. 1870)

The Mistletoe Bough, unsigned lithograph printed as a supplement
to *The Star,* December 1, 1838.

Would That Christmas Lasted the Whole Year Through

Christmas time! That man must be a misanthrope indeed, in whose breast something like a jovial feeling is not roused—in whose mind some pleasant associations are not awakened—by the recurrence of Christmas. There are people who will tell you that Christmas is not to them what it used to be; that each succeeding Christmas has found some cherished hope, or happy prospect, of the year before, dimmed or passed away; that the present only serves to remind them of reduced circumstances and straitened incomes—of the feasts they once bestowed on hollow friends, and of the cold looks that meet them now, in adversity and misfortune. Never heed such dismal reminiscences. There are few men who have lived long enough in the world, who cannot call up such thoughts any day in the year. Then do not select the merriest of the three hundred and sixty-five, for your doleful recollections, but draw your chair nearer the blazing fire—fill the glass and send round the song—and if your room be smaller than it was a dozen years ago, or if your glass be filled with reeking punch, instead of sparkling wine, put a good face on the matter, and empty it off-hand, and fill another, and troll off the old ditty you used to sing, and thank God it's no worse. . . .

from *Sketches by Boz* (1836) by Charles Dickens

Engraving in *Fairy Tales* by Hans Christian Andersen, 1900.